I AM Media Books Presents:

Born to be a Princess

Created by:
Princess Yehudah

ISBN: 978-1-951667-15-3

Published by I AM Media Books, Michigan, USA

Media to Awaken the World!

www.iammediabooks.com

I AM Media Books

This book is dedicated to all Judah Princesses across the globe.

Princess of Judah. Did you know you are:
"a crown of glory in the hand of God", a royal seed? (Isaiah 62:3)
"Sit down now, and read" (Jeremiah 36:15)

"These things have I written unto you that believe" (1 John 5:13)
"Thou shalt guide me with thy counsel, and afterward receive" (Psalm 73:24)

"Yet hear the word of God
O ye women, and let your ear receive the word of his mouth,
and teach your daughters wailing, and every one her
neighbour lamentation." (Jeremiah 9:20)

"And thy seed shall be as the dust of the earth, and thou shalt spread abroad to the west, and to the east, and to the north, and to the south:" (Genesis 28:14)
"And ye shall be unto me a kingdom of priests, and an holy nation." (Exodus 19:6)

"The wolf also shall dwell with the lamb, and the leopard shall lie down with the kid; and the calf and the young lion and the fatling together; and a little child shall lead." (Isaiah 11:6)

"In the beginning God created the heaven and the earth." (Genesis 1:1)

"Make me to understand the way of thy precepts: so shall I talk of thy wondrous works." (Psalm 119:27)

A "princess among the provinces;" (Lamentations 1:1)
That's who you were born to be.

"Honour thy father and thy mother: that thy days may be long upon the land which the LORD thy God giveth thee." (Exodus 20:12)

"Then said I, Ah, LORD God! behold, I cannot speak: for I am a child."
(Jeremiah 1:6)

"Hear the word of the LORD, O ye nations, and declare it in the isles."
(Jeremiah 31:10)

"Say not, I am a child: for thou shalt go to all that I shall send thee." (Jeremiah 1:7)
"Behold now, I have taken upon me to speak." (Genesis 18:27)

Daughter, you were created "in his own image, in the image of God" (Genesis 1:27)

"I AM THAT I AM." (Exodus 3:14)

"Put on the whole armour of God, that ye may be able to stand."
(Ephesians 6:11)

You were born to be a princess. "Behold an Israelite indeed." (John 1:47)
"I establish my covenant with you, and with your seed," (Genesis 9:9)

"Return unto the land of thy fathers, and to thy kindred;
and I will be with thee." (Genesis 31:3)
"Who can find a virtuous woman? for her price is far above rubies."   (Proverbs 31:10)

"The king's daughter is all glorious within:" (Psalm 45:13)
You were born to be a Princess.
"His seed shall be mighty upon earth: the generation of the upright shall be blessed."

(Psalm 112:2)

"Yea, I will make many people amazed."   (Ezekiel 32:10)

"Favour is deceitful, and beauty is vain:
but a woman that feareth the LORD, she shall be praised."   (Proverbs 31:30)

"I heard the voice of the LORD, saying, Whom shall I send, and who will go for us? Then said I, Here am I; send me." (Isaiah 6:8)
"Thus shalt thou say unto the children of Israel, I AM hath sent me." (Exodus 3:14)

"Awake, awake; put on thy strength, O Zion" (Isaiah 52:1)
"Blessed be the LORD my strength, which teacheth my hands to war,
and my fingers to fight:" (Psalm 144:1)

"Hear, O Israel: the LORD our God is one LORD:
And thou shalt love the LORD thy God with all thine heart,
and with all thy soul, and with all thy might." (Deuteronomy 6:4-5)

"I will make them to come and worship before thy feet, and to know that I have loved thee." (Revelation 3:9)
You were born to be a princess,
"He hath also stablished them for ever and ever: he hath made a decree." (Psalm 148:6)

"Judah, thou art he whom thy brethren shall praise." (Genesis 49:8)
"Now therefore thus saith the LORD of hosts; Consider your ways."
(Haggai 1:5)

Arise Israel! "I say unto thee, arise." (Mark 5:41)
"Love not sleep, lest thou come to poverty; open thine eyes," (Proverbs 20:13)
"For the LORD hath poured out upon you the spirit of deep sleep" (Isaiah 29:10)
"These see the works of the LORD, and his wonders in the deep." (Psalm 107:24)

"Judah mourneth, and the gates thereof languish; they are black unto the ground." (Jeremiah 14:2)
"Hold that fast which thou hast, that no man take thy crown." (Revelation 3:11)

"The sceptre shall not depart from Judah, nor a lawgiver from between his feet, until Shiloh come; and unto him shall the gathering of the people be." (Genesis 49:10)

"And the light of Israel shall be for a fire, and his Holy One for a flame."
(Isaiah 10:17)
You were born to be a princess, "I have even called thee by thy name:
I have surnamed thee, though thou hast not known me." (Isaiah 45:4)
Daughter of the "Lord of lords, and King of kings"; (Revelation 17:14)
That's who you were born to be!

The Ten

I
Thou shalt have no other gods before me.

II
Thou shalt not make unto thee any graven image.

III
Thou shalt not take the name of the Lord thy God in vain.

IV
Remember the sabbath day, to keep it holy.

Commandments

V
Honour thy father and thy mother.

VI
Thou shalt not kill.

VII
Thou shalt not commit adultery.

VIII
Thou shalt not steal.

IX
Thou shalt not bear false witness.

X
Thou shalt not covet.

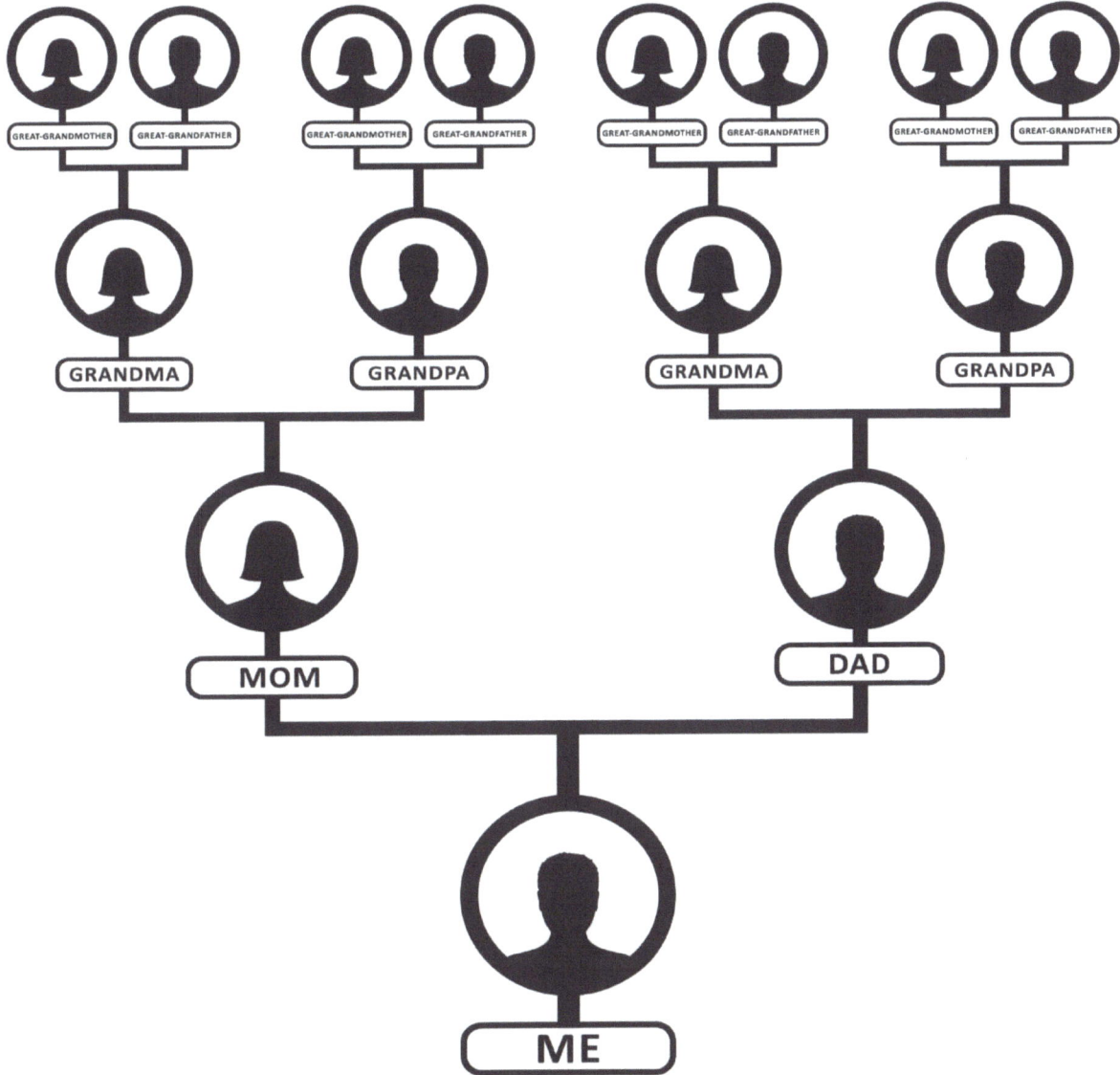

GREAT-GRANDMOTHER GREAT-GRANDFATHER GREAT-GRANDMOTHER GREAT-GRANDFATHER GREAT-GRANDMOTHER GREAT-GRANDFATHER GREAT-GRANDMOTHER GREAT-GRANDFATHER

GRANDMA GRANDPA GRANDMA GRANDPA

MOM DAD

ME

I LOVE MY FAMILY

About this Book

Born to be a Princess is a signature series by Princess Yehudah published by I AM Media Books. This series offers parents personalized, child-friendly tools to help teach beginning Bible readers to understand the Scriptures "precept upon precept; line upon line, line upon line; here a little, and there a little." (Isaiah 28:10)

Born to be a Princess: Beginning Bible Readers': Yehudah Edition is the first poetic personalized book in the series. This book uses God as the name of The Most High. You may elect to use the name of your choice in your personalized book. This book may also be persoanlized by tribe. For more information please check out:
www.iammediabooks.com

"For this cause also thank we God without ceasing, because, when ye received the word of God which ye heard of us, ye received it not as the word of men, but as it is in truth, the word of God, which effectually worketh also in you that believe."

(1 Thessalonians 2:13)

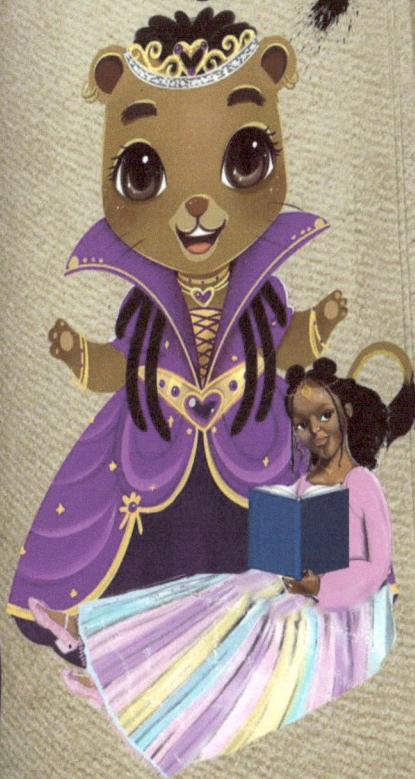

www.ingramcontent.com/pod-product-compliance
Lightning Source LLC
Chambersburg PA
CBHW040713280326

41926CB00083B/74